Oh, Sweet Revenge

by

John J. Olson

ISBN: 978-1-970024-77-7

Dedication

I dedicate this book to my niece
Abbie Passantino
and my sister
Alice Passantino.

Introduction

What happened that I am back again on death row? My life on the outside was marked by something that couldn't or shouldn't be left unfinished. This time I really deserve to be here. Why? Because I finally have gotten my sweet revenge. This is the story about the twenty-seventh prisoner being transferred from Alcatraz in 1963: twenty-six prisoners were recorded—this man, for some reason, was not. He tells his story as he lived it. Just remember this is only a story; the part about the transfers is accurate.

As I walk down this last mile I have time to reflect on and not regret of something. I regret that the first go-around I received wasn't really deserved. But this time I made damn sure it was earned and deserved.

I am walking down this last mile of my life because of four counts of murder. Of course I did these things; I felt justified but the law doesn't see it that way. Yet I am walking down it with my head held high. To the law I am just another animal not fit for society as we know it. They also say that the crimes I committed were unfounded.

But to my way of thinking I was still due some more justice, and it was definitely owed me. Actually as I think of it, that count should be five, starting with Sal Molino which I was blamed for and then the problematic one, my wife, which started the downfall of my life. Just stop to think of the things that run through your mind, as you know you only have the very last moments of your life. Thoughts like what could I have done differently? How did I ever get into this position that sent me over the edge?

I guess I have to remember the past as it all came about. But the closer I get to my demise the more I am in deep thought. I softly hear the priest saying something or another. I'm really not sure what the warden is saying next to him explaining the procedure to me. But that is all irrelevant now. All I know is that I am about to die. Am I ready? Yes, I think I am ready. But let me tell you how it all began, speaking with a reporter from a local newspaper, since I have returned to the United States to be executed for my crimes. His name is Gary Saltwell.

He is writing my life story, promising to locate my children and sharing the profits from the book sales—that is, if there are any profits to be had with them.

Chapter One

The Beginning

My name is Jake McFarland. I started out just like any other Joe straight out of college. I was about to become a certified public accountant. (This was my choice.) My parents, all they saw was a doctor, lawyer, or something along that line for me, but that was their choice. Well, you know that story. As I was saying, it all starts when I was twenty-three years old. I had met and fell in love with Grace.

When I first saw Grace I really knew in my heart that she was going to be my wife. We dated for a while and in 1948 we were going to be married. We had a June ceremony and the reception. It was a nice get-together. It was at that moment I realized that things would somehow be different now with a wife. I had a job with a small company which only paid $125.00 per week.

We had two lovely children. A boy named Thomas born in 1949, and the next year we had a little girl whom we named Felicia. We lived in a small apartment that was called railroad rooms. This consisted of four rooms and a bath. When you walked through the door you could see the whole apartment. It consisted of a kitchen with a bathroom at the end of it and two bedrooms and a living room on the other end of it. It also had a door in the living room to exit if you needed to.

As I said I was working for this small company as an accountant making $125.00 per week. Well at least it was a step in the right direction. We lived modestly to say the least. But we lived as well as anyone could during these times. My wife was never satisfied.

She soon became a bitch with a capital B. All she could do was keep complaining about this and that. Nothing seemed to be good enough anymore. She always wanted more. She seemed envious of everything and of everyone. Thus the fights started to mount about not managing to provide what they needed to enjoy life. She couldn't afford new clothes and other things like going out and throwing parties. I felt that living beyond our means was crazy.

It was now 1954 and the job wasn't really going anywhere. There was no promotion in sight. With the first child in school and the second preparing for kindergarten, things had to get better. Somehow we were just barely surviving the way things were at this point.

Grace also complained that she couldn't invite our friends to visit over in such a ratty apartment. I knew that I could have found something better somewhere else, but I was just starting out and didn't know all of the ropes. Not even sure where else I could go. I was making minimal raises but it just never seemed enough to satisfy our needs, no less extras. But Grace never understood that part.

The kids were growing up and they needed more things for their schooling, not to mention our lifestyle was stagnant to say the least. All the arguments started to get to me. I always seemed to be tired and on edge all the time. I soon found myself taking longer to get home at night. I started making excuses to get home later as time went on. I loved my wife and family, but all the fights occurring nightly had us all on edge.

If only I could figure this entire thing out. I am an educated man, but why couldn't I come up with an answer to my problems?

I soon started to stop by this bar near the house to have a few beers to calm down from work and prepare myself for the nightly ordeal that was inevitably to come along. My life just seemed to descend more and more into a rut, what with the daily work routine and the constant confusion at the home front. I started to really hate my career, which I so badly pursued for my life. I also started hating going home altogether. I really wanted so much for my life to drastically change somehow. But what could I do? My wife at this point was talking about leaving me and taking my children with her. I just couldn't allow this to happen.

I started to look for a better paying job in the same field, but there just didn't seem to be anything out there that was to be had. Anything else available at this time would have paid me a lot less than I was already making.

Time seemed to drag as it all seemed to be falling apart right in front of my eyes. Whatever ideas came to me, there always seemed to be a road block that would jump in the way. The needs for the home and the children seemed to increase quicker than I could provide for them.

I started to borrow from my friends and family hoping to be able to stretch it out as far as I could. But this also came to a complete halt. It seemed to be a nightmare just trying to survive living here on the coast: the cost of living was becoming unbearable. I had to think quickly or be ready to lose everything that I worked and breathed for.

But now all of the ideas that came to me seemed to dissipate just as quickly as it came. I was lost. My drinking was getting more frequent. But not in a bad way, but just more constant. I was almost ready to call the whole marriage and job quits. Unable to come up with any sort of resolution or anything else to resolve my problems, I couldn't cope with the aggravation much longer.

Chapter Two

A Proposition

Stopping in the bar one night after work and having quite a few bottles of beer, I started talking to this gentleman sitting next to me. He said his name was Sammy Merino. I introduced myself and we started to talk about nothing in particular as we drank. After quite a few rounds we were sharing things about our families and life in general. Before I knew it, I was telling Sammy about my problems at work and later my problems at home seemed to come out as well.

I explained that no matter how much I was making, it never seemed to be enough for the needs of our family to live on. After I mentioned that I was an accountant, he said, "Oh, a person working with numbers and books." I laughed and said, "Correct."

He told me he had an uncle who ran a company that needed a good bookkeeper with my knowledge. He mentioned that it was a business of imports and exports. He gave me an address down by the docks which was—right across from the island of Alcatraz. We continued talking about families and things in general the rest of the evening. It was turning into a pleasant evening all around.

I started trying to talk about the job and what my responsibilities would be, but Sammy kept changing the subject. He explained that I will find out after I talked with his uncle who owned the company, so I just let it go at that. Soon I said goodnight. After I left the bar, I thought it strange that Sammy kept changing the topic whenever I mentioned the job's responsibilities. I should have picked up that something was amiss, but I figured that I was so excited over the untimely yet so much needed opportunity, that I simply let all of the obvious slip by me. I felt that a giant weight was being lifted off my shoulders for some reason.

I decided to take a leisurely walk home. I thought it would be nice to maybe bring home some flowers, something which I rarely did of late. Grace surely would be surprised. Maybe, just maybe, we can have a peaceful evening for a change. I went home and told Grace about the man Sammy and about my interview tomorrow morning. This was the first time I saw a smile on her face in quite a long time. Grace really liked the flowers as she rarely got flowers from me anymore. We just couldn't afford them anymore.

I told her that this might be what we were waiting for. We sat and ate our dinner as a family. Oh god, I don't remember how long it's been since we sat down as a family. It sure seemed like ages ago. I really slept well that night for a change. I woke up invigorated for once, the best that I felt in quite a while.

Even Grace had this look on her face as if the world was now lifted off our shoulders. She knew that I would qualify for the job. Just think how I would look and feel if I got the job. We just had to think positively about the whole thing. I kissed Grace and the children good-bye and left for the interview. It was such a nice morning so I decided to walk instead of taking the trolley.

As I walked I was thinking of what to say to this man concerning my experience for the position which he needed filled. Would I have all the qualifications that he was looking for? I really only had worked for this small company, and would what I did there meet the needs for this company? I did know that I kept up with all of the new and so-called improvements for my area of expertise.

I didn't even know how in-depth with the financial aspects of the corporation I would be handling myself. I was soon to find out, though that was for sure if I got the job. All I knew about the company was that it was into import and export. Hell, I didn't even know the owner's name. I was so excited about the interview I forgot to ask Sammy what his name was. Well, it wasn't long before I saw the building at the end of the block.

I looked to my left and there was the prison. It seemed like it was staring at me. I don't know but I got an eerie feeling when I looked over there. It looked so big and dismal. Well, I better get a move on for my interview. Boy, talk about being nervous. I never realized the importance that prison had in store for my life....

Chapter Three

Job Interview

I was a little early for my interview. I had all the appropriate documents. Sammy's uncle arrived and you could tell that they were related. He shook my hand and said that his name was Sal Molino. I knew that I heard that name before but couldn't place it. He had me sit down and asked the usual questions. Was I married? Where did I go for college? He also asked about how much experience I had and what made me think he should hire me. I thought this was a question not really asked, but Sal seemed to be satisfied with my answers.

He explained some of the details of the position that I was being hired for. I asked him if I was hired. All he said was, "What do you think?" To be honest I really didn't know for sure, the way the interview went. Sal just looked at me and laughed a little. Then he asked me, "When would you like to start?" I told him, "As soon as possible." He answered that I was to report on Monday. That I would be on a trial basis, to see how I fit in with the company and the workload.

Sal said that I would start with a salary of $1,500 per week with benefits. Also, I'd have the use of a company vehicle. I was so happy with the news I thanked him and said that I would be there on Monday. It was the spring of 1954, the money was definitely great for that time. If I would have thought it through, I probably would have realized that something was wrong with it. But I didn't do that.

I went home and told Grace of our good fortune. She was happy and we finally went out to celebrate something good for a change. We got a babysitter and everything. We went to a fancy restaurant with a live band, the works.

We laughed and danced the night away. It felt like we were just married again. What a wonderful feeling that was.

Things were finally taking a turn for the better. The job was going well; even our marriage had taken a turn for the better. I was doing the usual accounting work including the payroll. After the first six months I was called into the office, which took me by surprise. I sure hoped that I wasn't getting the heave-ho. It turned out to be the opposite: Sal told me that he was satisfied with my work. Also that he was raising my salary to $3,000 per week. I just looked at him and he said that I was doing great. He also said that he was sure that I would earn every penny of it. I wondered what he meant by that statement. It was then that I realized Sal was probably tied into the mob somehow, but told myself my being their accountant was just another job to me.

We would surely now be able to move to Alameda. One of our dreams will now be there for us. Now the children will be able to have their own rooms. The times were finally changing for us. We would also have a pretty large yard, so that we could invite our friends over and entertain for the first time in our marriage.

Tommy was in the first grade and Felicia was in kindergarten. Tommy was now six and Felicia was just five when it all started to go downhill for Grace and me. The more I made, it seemed, Grace always wanted so much more. I always felt that I couldn't provide her with enough to satisfy all her needs or her wants. What I mean is I took us out of the slum we lived in and was making our lives better. Soon we became members of the local yachting club and we now seemed to know all the right people, but to no avail, she always wanted more and more. It was always more and more.

She would always complain this wasn't right or we didn't have this or that. But no matter, we were surviving. We weren't borrowing money anymore. We were making it on our own. No more bill collectors banging on the door either. Yes, we were on our way, if Grace would only be happy. That was one of my main objectives right now: to see to that no matter the cost.

All too soon it became my downfall. Grace had the fever, the lust for money. Her need to be accepted by her friends soon took over her as she now wanted maids and cooks. She also wanted to have a chauffeur to drive her around all day. My life was soon right back into the shit I put up with when we were first married. No let down whatsoever.

But still after eight years of marriage I was so in love with this woman. I couldn't think straight. I also knew that in order to save our marriage together, I had to come up with a plan. But what could I do? I thought about it for a while and figured that since I worked with the books, I could devise a scheme of how to fudge the numbers so no one would suspect that anything was going on.

I started out on a small scale of a thousand dollars per week. They were bringing in about twenty-two-and-a-half million per week. I figured it was just a drop in the bucket for them. But after about six months Grace started to bitch again about things not being up to her expectations. She wasn't exactly where she wanted to be in her circle of friends.

All I seemed to do was meet her demands without question or any concern of my well-being. After all I was so deep within the mob, I just couldn't think straight anymore. What I should have done was tell Grace to knock it off. But as always my heart overruled my head. I thought that maybe if I increased the take up to five thousand I would be safe enough. Maybe then Grace would be happy with the amount, so that she could now live in the style that she thinks she deserves.

Things started to really go downhill for me in all aspects of my life. My morale was down and I felt like I was drowning. Even while I seemed to be suffocating, my life felt as if I was being snuffed out like a candle. I knew that what I had done was irreversible and that all of this couldn't be repaired. Time sped by and after a year I thought that maybe, just maybe, it would be all right. Sal seemed to get worried about the books as he came to me one day and told me that the corporation was coming down within the next two weeks. That they were going over the books checking for what they thought were shortages.

I knew what had to be done: I was going to have to confront Sal before the next two weeks. There was no way I could ever replace that amount of money. Also, there was no way I could undo what I had done. I couldn't even think of a way to cover all this up. I finished up work for the day and replaced the books in the safe.

I decided to stop at the bar for a few drinks before I headed for the house. I had about three or four drinks and then left for home.

Everyone was eating dinner when I arrived, so I sat in my place at the table and Grace brought me my dinner. We ate as usual in silence except for a little bit of chit-chat about our day. The next day at work wasn't too exciting so I wrapped it up for the day. I decided to spend some time with Grace and the children. We went for a drive and then picked up some takeout on the way home. The kids always liked takeout for dinner.

We arrived home and the kids ate dinner and got ready for their baths. There was school tomorrow. After the kids got to bed, Grace and I sat around and talked before turning in ourselves. I had to be in work early the next day. The days at work seemed more troublesome as of late, as I tried to figure out the best way to approach Sal. At this point I really couldn't figure out how to explain this to anyone no less Sal.

I really didn't feel like going home right then, so I started walking my usual route and tried to figure out where and when this entire mess all started. I guess it all started when I stopped in for a drink a few years back. I mean there were plenty of bars in the area, why did I pick this particular bar? Was this to be my fate so many years ago?

Who would have thought that I would become just another embezzler? Or even that I would be involved with the mob? Was this all predestined that long ago and there would be no return? No return at least to my knowledge. I did know one thing for sure: I couldn't do this anymore. I did have about twenty grand tucked away that Grace didn't know about. It was for emergency purposes and this surely fit the description. I guess that all I could do was act as if it was business as usual around the house, though I did know that this wouldn't last long. Most times I felt that my problems on the home front were as bad as my work problems have become. The next couple of days went by without incident.

I again found the urge to stop for a few drinks before going home. Also to try and think of some way to wind all of this down and be finished with it. The bar was quiet when I arrived and I sat in my usual place. The bartender brought me my usual drink, a Dewar's and water with a twist. He asked me if Sammy had caught up with me. I told him no and asked him why. All he said was that Sammy stopped in and asked if I had been in lately that's all. I asked him if Sammy mentioned why he was looking for me.

No he answered, then asked me if I was in some kind of trouble. He knew who I was working for, but I told him no but that it must be something, though. He smiled and said okay that I didn't need any trouble with them guys. I said that I knew what he meant but thanks everything was all right. I finished my drink and decided to leave. Saying my goodnights and leaving him a tip I left the bar.

I finally realized that my life as I knew it was really in trouble. I couldn't even see any light at the end of the tunnel for me. An idea crossed my ragged mind that maybe I could run. Would Grace go if I asked her? Could we and the kids just disappear and no one would find us? But where would be far enough to really lose ourselves? The children would have to go to school somewhere. All of our lives will have to be uprooted and changed. There would never be coming back to the life we have become used to that would be for sure.

I would have to continue to work. I seemed to be grasping at straws. Would there be a place so distant that we could really be safe? I think not. I don't even know for sure if Grace would even consider it. That would be my biggest question. This entire if-and-what-nots isn't getting me anywhere that is one thing for sure.

Maybe Grace would surprise me and consider my idea. It would surely surprise me to think that she would really go for this new life that seems to be dumped in my, all of our laps. All because of my stupidity to please her: I decided not to even go that route, because of her negative attitude about anything that has to do with me.

Chapter Four

Dealing with the Problem

I continued on my walk home the long way, because I had to figure something out in a hurry. I walked for hours and still made no headway. I figured that I better get home. The house was quiet; everyone was asleep as it was really late. I didn't even know that I walked that long. I got myself ready and went to bed. I slept restlessly and woke up in a cold sweat, but then that seemed to be the norm lately. I got ready for work, kissed Grace and the kids goodbye, and started for the office. The day seemed to go as it always did, just another day. I finally figured out what I had to do in hopes of making it right, if that was possible at this late date: I had to confront Sal with it.

For some stupid reason I thought it would work out. I didn't know what I was going to say and also didn't know what the response would be. All I did know was that I had to do something. How do they say it? "Let the chips fall and see how they lay." I went to the bar to try and get prepared for what was the inevitable moment. I seemed to need fortification. I sat and all the while muttering to myself about what I was planning to do when I got in to see Sal. After an hour or so I felt that I was fortified enough to go and see Sal. I finished my drink and left the bar. I was so nervous I felt my legs wobbling. I told myself to calm down or Sal would see right through me. The closer I got to Sal's office building the worse I felt. There was no turning back now that was for sure. Well maybe he will listen to reason, then again maybe not. I really didn't want to know what would happen if he didn't agree with me. I got a chill as I approached Sal's building.

I figured that I better get in there and see Sal and explain it to Him. I just hoped that he would understand what I was going through. Other wives were probably no different from mine was. Not that it made what I did right by any means. I waited until I was sure that Sal would be alone, as I didn't want any interference. As I entered the building all I could hear was silence. No, let me correct that: I could only hear the pounding of my heart; it sounded deafening in the quiet hallway. I walked towards Sal's office and listened; there was silence He was alone. I knocked on the door and was asked to come in. All I heard was "What do you want, Jake?" Sal didn't even look up; it was as if He expected me.

I didn't even know how or where to start. But start I did.

"Sal, I have this problem and I need to clear it up."

"It's a little too late for that, isn't it, Jake? I trusted you. I trusted you, Jake, and I treated you as my own family and this is what I get in return? You stole from me, not only that you stole from my family."

"Sal, I am sorry. I had financial problems and couldn't bail myself out. Grace was hounding me to do better and I loved her so much, but she always wanted more and more. No matter how much I provided it seemed never enough. Sal, I was sure that you would understand. You're married and know what it's like."

"No, Jake! I don't know what it's like you—tell me. 'Cause wives in the family respect their husbands and they know their place. But you can't blame your wife, Jake. You stole from me and not your wife. No not your wife, Jake. You stole I figure about one and a half million dollars of my money. The family wants it back or I'll have to close your account permanently. Now do you understand, Jake?"

"'Close my account'? What does that mean?"

"It means to cancel your Christmas."

"But, but I need time. I can't settle that all at once."

That's when I saw it, the gun Sal was holding in his hand. I knew in my heart that I had to move quickly. I jumped across the table and grabbed for the gun. We struggled and that is when I heard it go off.

I never heard a louder sound in my life. I looked at Sal and He looked back at me while slumping over the desk.

I was shaking and couldn't grasp what had just happened. All I could think of was that I was really in deep shit now. My life would be worth nothing. I tried to think of what I would tell Grace and would she understand? I know I had to run for it. Run! But run where? I went to the safe which was open and took out about thirty grand in cash. I figured I might need it until I knew what I was going to do.

I quickly went home and parked the car around the block, then I walked to the house and entered through the garage where I had the other money that I had been hiding just in case. I figured that I would fly somewhere far enough away where they (the mob) or the law wouldn't find me The cops as well as the mob would probably be hunting me by now. After I grabbed the money, I thought that I would check on the kids and Grace before I left. They were all asleep, which was for the best. This way I wouldn't have to explain anything. I had a bag prepared just in case of a problem in which I would have to leave suddenly. Sometimes our life plans doesn't seem to work out the way it should, and you always are the one left on the short end of the stick. I left a note for Grace and about fifteen thousand dollars to tide her over until I could get in touch with her again.

I seemed to hear sirens in the distance; the sounds seemed to be getting closer. I quickly got into my car and hightailed it to the airport. If the mob got ahold of me I'd be dead for sure. I couldn't figure out which would be the lesser evil of the two. I drove around for a while and parked my car and hailed a taxi to take me to the airport. This way if the police saw my car they would think I was still around the city. I knew that the mob wouldn't find out until Sal's body was discovered. But I did know that they sure as hell would be looking as soon as they did find out about it.

As my ideals and plans now will be forsaken, I arrived at the airport, paid my fare, and tipped the cabdriver. I then went in and ordered my ticket then checked in at the gate. Gate twenty-three was bound for Europe. My plane was being delayed and would be departing at 11:00 p.m. It was now around eight-thirty. I thought that I would go into the lounge and have a couple of drinks to settle my nerves before the flight. I really didn't want to be in the open for any length of time; between the police or the mob I didn't know which one would be worse. Then again I didn't really want to find out. I sat for a few hours and after three drinks or four I seemed to have lost count. My mind was so wrapped up in my problems that I couldn't really think straight. But it was just comforting to sit in the quiet lounge for a while!

My mind was wandering as to where I would wind up or what would I do when I got there. All I did know was that my whole life would be changed. But the first thing was to be somewhere that I could start a new life for myself. I did wonder, though, if I would always be looking over my shoulder for the rest of my life.

Chapter Five

My Departure

Before I knew it they were calling my flight. I was to report to the gate. I finished my drink, left a nice tip, and cautiously approached the boarding area's gate. I was hoping to get unto the plane quickly. That wasn't meant to happen, though. I handed my boarding pass to the agent and was promptly told that my flight had been canceled. I questioned it, and then I saw two men approaching with their badges already out.

They approached me and asked if I was Jake McFarland. I replied by asking who they were and what did they want. They told me that they were from the United States Treasury Department, that they had some questions to ask me. They then took me upstairs to a small room; the windows were barred and there was only a table and a few chairs around it. They started to grill me about my life, marriage, and about the job. They asked me if I had embezzled the money. I replied, "Yes, I did embezzle the money." They wanted to know if I killed my boss in the heated argument. I told them it was an accident. They asked if it wasn't murder why was I running. That was when I knew that my life as I knew it was gone for sure. I wondered how they knew about it already.

I requested to have a lawyer present. They replied that if I was innocent, what did I need a lawyer for? I wasn't really sure but figured that I should have one present. It was around midnight, so I used my one phone call and called a lawyer friend of mine. He came down to the airport and was directed to where I was. I explained the situation to him as it unfolded in my life. He explained that this wasn't his field of expertise, but there was this lawyer friend of his who was a criminal lawyer. We spoke to the treasury agents and we explained what happened with the gun and the money problem.

I didn't want to let too much of the story out because of the fear of retaliation towards my family or myself. I knew the mob would be after me but I didn't want my family touched either. I was told that I would be safe during the procedures and the trial, but I was concerned about my family: would they be in danger? I was assured that they would be moved to a safe place. I answered the questions they continued to ask me. Well at least the ones that my lawyer friend would let me answer. The agents got the gist that I was finished for the time being and transferred me to a secure location where I would be housed for the duration of the proceedings out of fear of retaliation from the mob which would be so ever present.

Just think that all I ever wanted to do in life was to raise my family and live a normal and happy life with my wife. Now all that seemed to be gone forever. After a while I'd gotten settled into the place where I and the agents would be housed. My friend left after telling me that he would return in the morning with the other lawyer. That is if the other lawyer wanted to see me. They showed me the room I would be in and then I settled down for the night. I couldn't sleep; I just tossed and turned with a million thoughts going through my head at once. Morning came quickly with nothing resolved.

There came a knock on the door and one of the agents asked if I was up and wanted anything to eat. Gee, I didn't even think about food for at least twenty-four hours, I was starving. I said that I was up and would shower first; afterwards I went to the living room. The first thing I smelled was fresh coffee brewing. It was then that I finally realized how hungry I really was. The food was excellent and I was happy to have eaten finally. Soon my lawyers arrived; the two agents were also present. There also was a detective, and someone from the prosecutor's office arrived.

I was officially arrested for the murder of Sal Molino, embezzlement, and income tax evasion. Only then was I allowed to talk to my new lawyer, a Mister Robert F. Goodwin.

I explained to him what and exactly how it all happened. All he did was take notes and informed me that I didn't have to talk to anyone else unless he was present at the time. I then called the house and explained it all to Grace, who wasn't very happy to say the least at this point. The lawyer and I went back into the room where the others were waiting. Another person had entered the room in our absence. It was a woman with some sort of a machine; she turned out to be the stenographer. She would be taking down the whole question-and-answer part during proceedings.

The morning went as expected, long and strenuous. We finally broke for lunch and I asked my lawyer what he thought. He told me it didn't look easy that was for sure. Also that all three of the charges were heavy duty time; I asked if my wife could come and was told that someone would bring her. For safety reasons, the afternoon session was as grueling as the morning session was. By the end of the questioning I was told that my wife had arrived and I could see her shortly. I asked if my children were there also. I was promptly told they weren't.

The visit went as I thought it would go—with me explaining and her yelling and screaming. All she was worried about was how she was going to survive this ordeal. I promptly reminded that it was my ass on the line, not hers. She then went on about how she would now have to get a job. The only thing that didn't seem to affect her was my problem. If I would spend my life in prison or if I would be put to death was of no concern of hers; it seemed as if I had become nonexistent in her life. Grace started to scream and shout. The agent knocked on the door asking if everything was okay. I called out that my wife was upset. That was the understatement of the day.

I asked how the children were handling the situation and was told that she told them I had to take a trip. I asked her to tell them that Daddy loved them. I knew she wouldn't do that. I felt that our little visit was over at this point and called for the agent to please show her out. She yelled back something about suing me for everything I had. This to me was practically zero at this point.

The next few weeks seemed to never end with questions from all sides. Did I plan to kill Sal Molino? Why did I need to steal the money over such a long period? What was my relationship with the mob? All these questions was answered and reanswered, but it seemed that my answers weren't what they seemed to be going to accept. The questioning process seemed to get longer and longer each day. My answers really didn't change from the beginning, but they still hammered away. I finally came up with the answer: they just wanted to see if I would trip up somewhere along the line. I really wanted to get out of the safe house sometimes soon, but that wasn't in the cards.

I was told that I would be appearing in court in a week or two as soon as there was a clearing on the court's docket. My lawyer told me that within a few days I would be going out for some clothes that would be more appropriate for the court proceedings. I marveled at my first trip since I was arrested. Just think how a breath of fresh air would mean so much to a person. I waited for that day to come, like a child would wait for Christmas morning to arrive. The day finally came and I was led to a limousine surrounded by six agents. I felt like I was someone of importance instead of a CPA-turned-criminal.

It was going to be an interesting day outside, a day without the question-and-answer sessions I had become accustomed to. We drove for what seemed like hours and I realized that they were taking me out of the Bay Area for safety reasons. That was totally reasonable to me.

We drove north to some town and the agents got out of the limo and checked all around. We were in some shopping area; when they were assured it was safe they returned to get me. We entered the building, which resembled some shopping complex with a variety of store fronts.

There were a couple of men's shops there and we proceeded to go shopping. I picked out a couple of suits, a couple of shirts and ties, and some other personal items. Next we went to the men's shoe store. I picked out two pair of shoes and a pair of slippers.

After we were done shopping, they took me to a nice restaurant for lunch. Now that was a special treat. I didn't mind the meals in the safe house, but some of the cooking was something to be desired.

All good things must come to an end. So did my day trip. I guessed that it was now going to be soon for my trial since they had me get all these new duds. I didn't know if I was anxious or just so nervous that I was experiencing this entire sort of anxiety all of the time. All I did know was that I was glad it was going to start soon.

Chapter Six

The Awaited Trial

The process of the law always amazed me at how slow or how swiftly it had gone when it needed to. All the procedures you had to go through to reach a common goal. The length of time spent for the interrogation is way beyond comprehension. My lawyer tried to get my statements and witnesses for me, but that was hard considering the situation I was in.

The prosecutor's office had this young lawyer ready to make a name for himself. His name was Jason Gibbs. The judge was one of those hard noses you always heard about and you prayed that you'd never get. That is if you have to appear before one. But I got him, which was the way things seemed to be going for me. His name was Albert B Conklin. I felt that I needed a miracle to save me. The court date was soon on the horizon. I was real tired of being cooped up in the safe house. I couldn't go anywhere, not that I really had anywhere to go.

We prepared for the trial; the main thing going against me was I really had no one to use as a witness. No one except of course myself, which I figured wouldn't be of much help. The state held all the cards so to speak. They had the motive, the body, and also the gun. I finally resolved that my days as a free man were numbered as the court date arrived.

The courtroom wasn't what I expected it to be. It was rather dismal-looking, a cold room that looked like it was made of wood. It was a typical courtroom I guess. There was a jury, stenographer, the judge, and a bailiff. The court called my case on April 23, 1957, and it lasted until May22, 1957. As I figured, they convicted me on all counts. Count one was embezzlement, count two income tax evasion, and murder in the second degree was count three.

Sentencing would be held in two weeks. So here I was waiting again, only this time it was behind bars instead of a safe house. Just sitting behind bars got my mind to start working of what would happen, and about my wife, children, and just about everything outside of these walls and bars that now surround me. One seemed to get this feeling of encasement. It's like being wrapped in a cocoon or encased in a plastic bubble. On June third I was sentenced to life in prison.

There seemed to be absolutely no correspondence from the outside world, with the exception of my lawyer. My wife disappeared with my children, and my folks passed away within the last year. My friends, what few I did have, seemed not to answer any calls or letters that I had written. So here I was with no one to get any information from. My lawyer did stop by and he had divorce papers with him. I signed them reluctantly, but what else could I do at this point. I had nothing to offer now, nor would I have anything to offer them in the future. That's how it looked from my point of view. Besides, I didn't even know where they were. My lawyer had no knowledge of where they were or so he said.

I didn't know if I would ever see my children again. How I loved and missed them so much. The isolation in my life seemed to be all that was left. As the time went by I started to realize what my fate would be. The sentencing came and gone before I knew or felt it. Altogether I received a life sentence on all counts without the possibility of parole. I immediately asked for an appeal but while I awaited the decision I had been sent to the Rock. Yes! Alcatraz. Where I would be temporarily housed during the procedures, if granted.

Why the Rock? Well, I was told that it was the nearest to the court and it had vacancies. What a choice of words, as if it was an exclusive hotel in the area. All kinds of things were going through my head, adjusting to my present situation and thinking of my long-term plan. I guessed this was to be another one of those sleepless nights. I was becoming accustomed to them happening more often then.

Monday morning July 1, 1957 came and I went to the courthouse with my lawyer to plead my case for the appeal hearing. It was granted to me. I guessed that in the morning I would be going for another boat ride. I really had nothing to pack, so I would just say that I was ready for the trip. I didn't sleep too well that night. All these things came to me at once. All my questions seemed to bunch together and my mind was focused on memories of my family and the outside that was going to be left behind. Thoughts racked my brain, of questions like what if I didn't do this? Or what if I didn't need this or that to satisfy my and my wife's needs and demands? If it wasn't for the kids we probably wouldn't have been together, period.

I guessed that only time would tell. I wondered if there was any injustice done that I was unaware of that could be a decisive factor relevant to my cause, which was my freedom? I felt that if I could go back mentally to all that happened around and during the crimes for which I have been convicted of, that would help. Well I did know that I had quite a bit of time to figure it out. Would Goodwin find anything new that could possibly be of any help to my cause at all? I really hoped so. As of then I was in a state of mind that I couldn't even think straight.

I tried my best to get some sleep, but all these things kept coming into my head as if to forbid me to rest. I got up and washed myself, and then got dressed for what would be my last breakfast before going to the Rock. I was ready when the guard brought me the tray of food which consisted of cereal, a small container of milk, some toast and eggs which didn't seem too bad. I just about finished my breakfast when I heard the sound of keys from the hallway area; I was ready when the guards arrived to take me to my new residence. The short trip began. I guessed I would be coming back and forth to the appeals court when the appeals process began; would there be any possible way that I could find the needle in the haystack to have the court's decision overturned?

Chapter Seven

Arriving at the Rock

The guards arrived and told me to get myself ready for the trip. We arrived at the dock around 8:00 a.m. and had a short wait for the ferry, as it had just left with employees who lived off the prison grounds. It was a foggy morning and the island looked kind of grey and dismal. I thought it was due to the fog, but I was definitely dead wrong. I was told that was how it always looked. Soon we arrived at the dock which seemed like no time at all.

As I stood waiting to enter what would be my new home, I felt I must now succumb to what was to be my plight. I knew that my wife and children were definitely gone. I saw very little of trees and grass upon the island. It was nothing but gray rock; a smattering of brown and green moss surrounded the island in which I was about to stay. As we pulled into the dock, I noticed the children who lived on the island waiting to board the ferry to go to their classes on the mainland. A couple of the children waved and I smiled back to them, just think that they lived on this island too; after we docked we headed to the admissions area and went into the building. I was fingerprinted again. Next, to get my clothes and bedding, orientation, and physical examination.

After that I would be escorted to my cell block. The cell was about five feet by nine feet with a cot for my bed. It stood in front of the head (toilet) with a small sink that sat on the same wall as the toilet. Across from the bed was wooded tabletop and seat. It had to stay folded up to simulate some space within the confines of the cell.

I didn't think there was very much interior decorating that could be done with my cell. But then again I guessed it's not set up for comfort. The daily routine I had to endure was nothing but frivolous. There your surname or a number was how you were called. McFarland or 1759 in my case.

It was a far cry from Mr. McFarland or Jake that I was used to. All because of a big mistake, but that's all water under the bridge. There weren't any phones in the cells, and I really couldn't keep up with things going on with my appeal unless my lawyer came with news, which wasn't as often as I would have liked; but knowing the way the system worked, I know that I had to just grin and bear it, so to speak.

After going through the mandatory orientation, I was allowed to get a job in the laundry room. It paid a quarter an hour. This was definitely way less than what I was accustomed to making, but at least I was out of the cell and around people for the first time in weeks. Time on the Rock didn't seem to go as fast as you would like it to, but you just have to keep your mind busy and it did really pass. My job kept me occupied for much of the day. It's the downtime in the cell, where all one had to do was think. That was where the real hard time came in. That was the time that never seemed to end.

Getting adjusted to my environment was one of the hardest things I had to endure. There was no more communication from the outside world. Everything and everyone I had known or loved had disappeared. All I had left was my nonexistent life on the island. I stayed in touch with my lawyer to find out how he was making out with the appeal, but all he told me was that a thing like this took time, as we didn't have too much to go on or to add at this point. That I had to be patient! I think patience was about the only thing I had left in the world.

I did enjoy the times that I had outside. I could look out at the bay and watch the gulls as they looked for food on the water. One could watch them all day. They would search below the waters and swoop down to their prey. When and if there was any to be found, you could see them holding their captives in their beaks and flying to a place where they wouldn't be disturbed with their meal.

One made very few friends on the Rock, and if you did find one you would be lucky. The food wasn't as bad as people say it was; a bit bland but edible. I did start to catch up with my reading again. Over the years I seemed to get away from that. With all the responsibilities of family life, this was definitely a different world from what I had become accustomed to. This place was so much like a tomb. It was so quiet. No one was even allowed to talk with exception of the mess hall, or when you were outside in the yard. Well, actually it was called the big yard.

You were only allowed outside when the weather was good. During the week you were allowed out after breakfast and only until you went to your work detail. You were allowed outside after work for a while until dinner was ready to be served. Saturdays and Sundays you could spend a few hours in the big yard depending upon the weather or if there was a lockdown or you had a visit. At this time I had no visitors whatsoever.

The appeals seemed to take place with no resolve. As time passed so did my hopes of ever getting out of Alcatraz. The only visitors I received were a stray insect, an island mouse that would seek out warmth, and a morsel of food. They aren't too good with conversation but then again they were good listeners. They never objected to the topic, they just went about their business of eating whatever was available for them.

After two years I changed jobs and worked in the library sorting and shelving books donated from across the bay. The job was better than the laundry and I made thirty-five cents an hour. Another plus was that I was able to get first choice of the books I wanted as soon as they came in. There was definitely a vast variety of books to pick from. I found some that interested me concerning the law. I took a few and started to really read them. Not just read them, I devoured them in hopes that I could grasp a shred of light on my situation as it was at this point.

There wasn't much of a selection as it was a small library, but what was available was very informative. There were so many rules pertaining to the law and just about as many loopholes that would help to contest them, or even have them overruled. That is, if one really knew what he was doing. It seems you always have the lawyer who does his best so to speak, but could have actually done better. The way I looked at it, it was the case with my lawyer.

I figured that if I studied this, to the best of my knowledge, maybe I could figure out a way to get back on the outside. There had to be some flaw within the case, The United States vs. McFarland, if I could come up with something that could reopen the trial. There must be something?

I had this feeling and it wouldn't go away. I also knew I really didn't have too much to lose by trying. This new endeavor seemed to occupy my empty nights as it gave me something to think back on. This was like redoing a puzzle, to see if it would finish up differently from the first time.

Time was slowly passing and during my yard time I would just stand on the top seat of the cement bleacher like steps to stare across the bay. All the while the gulls kept flying and swooping down for the daily catch. I remained busy in the library, so my time was really fulfilled for the most part. My children were the only things in my life that I missed. I would never have the chance to see them grow up. This was the saddest part of this whole ordeal that was for sure. I didn't even know where they were at this point in my life. But it's certain that my first goal, if I were to leave here, would be to locate my children wherever they were. I thought that with my partial knowledge of the laws somehow, someway I might benefit from it. I read every chance I could get trying to gain much needed knowledge.

I grew more and more alone in this world as time crept by. Almost recluse like; here I was surrounded by people yet I was so alone. I also found that I was becoming a bitter man, mad at the world and at myself for getting into the situation I was in. The days seemed to become more stressful, the daily routine more cumbersome to say the least. My thoughts drifted to the outer world, beyond the walls and further beyond the island itself, to the much distant world and life I had let be taken from me. I wondered if I would ever regain part of what I had lost. I kept thinking where my children were and if they were all right. Thoughts of my wife faded as I really didn't care to ever see her again. The days, weeks, and months seemed to creep by slowly, yet the years seemed to fly by. Soon it was New Year's Day 1962. To me and others it didn't seem like much to celebrate about bringing in a new year on this island that's for sure. I thought, *June 3, 1963 I would be here five years. What the hell do I have to be happy about? No family or friends to be with to share the coming of a New Year with aspirations of good things to come.*

On the Rock it always seemed as if time stood still. We simply adjusted to whatever came along. The most excitement came from the monthly movie with the news reels and cartoons. The news reels were important because it allowed us to know what we were missing being in this prison. The only time we missed out on this was if we were on lockdown.

Chapter Eight

Rumors Starting

Rumors started to fly around the place that they were going to close the Rock because the cost to keep it open was getting out of hand. The guards would deny this but the inner grapevine from the other inmates kept relaying this message. Everyone wondered what would eventually happen to the prisoners who were still on the island. I would guess there were still around thirty prisoners, including me. Not too sure of the actual count, though. As all rumors go, there was also a time frame included—late 1962 or early in 1963. All that would be left to think about was where I was going from there. Quite a few prisons were being mentioned by the hacks (guards) and prisoners alike.

We knew there were a couple of newer prisons soon to be opening. The only thing left to reckon was who, when, and where we all would be transferred to. The prisons mainly mentioned were USP Terra Haute in Indiana, USP Leavenworth in Kansas, USP Lewisburg in Pennsylvania, another in Atlanta, Georgia, a newer one, FCI Milan Michigan, and there was San Quentin Prison.

Now at least we knew about where some of us would be going too. All we needed to know now was when and who was going where? So the days just seemed to go by, and everyone settled back into their daily routines. My spare time outside in the big yard was spent on the top tier of the stone like steps where the other inmates sat and chatted. It took time before a prisoner was awarded to take a seat on the top level. There, one can look over the tall fence that surrounded us across to the harbor of San Francisco.

As always the skies were filled with the gulls scouring the waters in search of their meal. Life for them seemed so simple compared to ours. Most days it was so foggy one couldn't even see the mainland, though it always was comforting to know that it was there. As I looked out at nothing in particular, I thought how freedom seems to be taken for granted by all of us. We don't realize what we have until we lose it.

Our freedoms are always pushed back in our way of life. Then when it's gone it all comes back and smacks one right in the face thinking of what we really lost.

Well at last the laundry list is out and posted in the eating area. The "laundry list" is a list of where each inmate will be going. We all looked to see who was going where. My name was all the way at the bottom of the list. Where I was going was a bunch of question marks. There was twenty-six transfers plus myself twenty-seven in all. This made me wonder.

All this waiting and I still hadn't a clue as to where I was to be transferred to. What was so hard about picking one of the facilities where inmates were to be transferred to? But no! That would be too easy. One of the guards sort of hinted that I might be going to Leavenworth, but it wound up being overcrowded. So I had to go to the Q., which was San Quentin Prison up in the northern part of the state. The time seemed to go slowly at times and faster on other days. Soon we were approaching the end of our time on the Rock. My thoughts were now focused on what I would come to expect when I arrived at my destination. Most prisons were the same: drab-looking, and there always was a coldness or dampness about the place. I guess what they say is true: that prisons weren't for one's enjoyment. Neither were they built for one's comfort. I am sure of that.

The day had arrived: March 21, 1963, the closing date of Alcatraz, the Rock. It was also my departure date. I guess that I should be honored being the last inmate leaving the Rock. What an honor. I will be known the world over for that honor. It was a short trip to San Quentin only about 18 miles to the north. I didn't even have time to think about anything of importance.

I spent nearly six years on the Rock. Now I will be starting over like a brand-new inmate. Like I said the trip would be a short one, but it was a pleasant trip as I knew where I was headed and what I could expect once I arrived. The morning had a brisk chill mixed in with the usual morning fog. I realized that I would get a new number, different cell, and probably a new job. I also heard that I would have to go through orientation all over. I would be given a new handbook of the prison rules and regulations. It was also mentioned that usual physical would have to be done. They said that I would be put into isolation for the intake assessment. This generally takes up to two weeks. After the intake I would be put into the initial classification phase followed by the placement that took six to eight weeks. The move went smoothly and my orientation was complete. That went well because it wasn't much different from the Rock.

I would be assigned to the medium security facilities because I wasn't an apparent flight risk or a troublemaker. But because of my sentence, that was the best I could receive here at the Q.

I was heading for the population area to my new home behind these walls. I would be starting a new job in the laundry until an opening in the library became available. I would be making $150 per month, equivalent to forty cents per hour. I didn't smoke so I won't have to worry about cigarettes. I didn't need much in here that's for sure.

I really was hoping to get that job in the library as soon as possible. I was looking forward to continue my attempt of getting my sentence overturned. But that had to be put on hold, as one was only allowed a book every two weeks; Because of that I really didn't have that special benefit of getting the best books like I did at the Rock.

There seemed to be a lot of jailhouse lawyers at the Q. "Jailhouse lawyers" was what they were called, or should I say "we" were called. I knew that soon I would be able to continue my quest for freedom. Life at the Q was different in many ways from residing at the Rock. The cells were about the same size, you had very little room for anything in them. I guess I could make myself comfortable here. I had to live with it for quite a while. Forever it seemed. Work at the laundry wasn't that bad. I could manage it that's for sure, it couldn't be that much different here.

The one thing that was different from the Rock was that the big yard was different. It didn't overlook the bay that I really enjoyed for its view. I could mentally escape my surroundings there. Well, I really did have to adjust to my new surroundings at the Q, but I would survive it. I knew that if I abided by the rules and regulations of the prison and the unofficial rules of the inmates I could make it here. Your time could be easy or it could be hard, it's what you make of it that counts. I soon met a guy named Joe G. who seemed to know the ropes there. Joe seemed like a dependable and likable person and we hit it off okay. He let me know the dos and don'ts of prison life at the Q. We became friends and enjoyed each other's company. I was inhaling everything I could learn about judicial law from the books and the other inmates as they explained what they thought all of the laws meant. My head was spinning half of the time.

But I did know that I was learning a lot more than I knew before. My thoughts drifted back to the beginning to try and figure out if it was all worth the effort that I had put into it or if I was just wasting my time. Only time would tell. Joe and I seemed to talk about everything under the sun. Our families both seemed to not have any left that bothered or cared about us. I never heard from my lawyer again and I didn't even care at this point. The only thing was that I believed he could have tried harder. But that all seemed to be water under the bridge now; the more I had gotten into my endeavor, the faster the time seemed to go by.

I spent a good part of twenty-one years analyzing, studying and storing in my brain all the laws past and present. Things seemed to be coming together in my mind. I did learn something that could change the whole conviction around. I found out that I was wrongfully convicted of murder. How simple it was. I was wondering why no one asked the question before.

But I did know I would definitely pursue it with everything I have learned. The question is whose fingerprints were on the gun? If I could prove that my fingerprints are nowhere on the gun. Then how could I be convicted of second degree murder? If this is the proof that I needed all along, it definitely would be worth the effort. My life seemed to mean something again. I also found out that the judge was tied to the mob, which meant that I didn't have a snowball's chance in hell of not being convicted. I did know one thing for sure: I needed to get out of this place.

I was starting to find out the whereabouts of all the people who were to blame for my incarceration. My list was short, but it was definitely necessary for my needs now; maybe some of the others were also tied in with the mob somehow.

Chapter Nine

Prepping for My Future

My list consisted of my wife Grace who lived somewhere in Italy. After our divorce she met and married Garret Giovani, a small-time mob figure. Another was Judge Albert B. Conklin who lived in the Bay area, living alone. He wasn't ever married. There was the prosecutor, Jason Gibbs, who lived in Fresno, CA. He was married with two children. My Lawyer Robert F. Goodwin lived in Stockton, CA. He was divorced. All that was left was to somehow get out of here.

I was talking to my friend Joe and another fellow named Pete about things in general when the conversation wound up to where it usually did, my case and my feelings towards the people involved. Joe had mentioned to me that he learned about this lawyer from another inmate; that this lawyer had made a reputation for himself by getting sentences overturned for people who had been wrongfully prosecuted. His name was Herman Santos. He lived in the area. I looked up his number and gave him a call. I explained my story to him and he said that he had heard about this judge. He also knew that the judge was definitely tied in with the mob.

Herman mentioned that we would definitely need the gun to prove that my prints weren't even on the gun. It would be new evidence that could get me a new trial and a new start outside of these walls. He said he would stop by the next day to go through all the information concerning the case. Mr. Santos came the following afternoon after lunch to discuss the case with me. We were escorted to a small room so we wouldn't be disturbed by the conversations of the other inmates with their visitors. After he had the necessary information he needed to start with, he left saying he would be back as soon as he had it altogether.

I couldn't get much sleep that night trying to figure out all the things that would be of help to us in our endeavor. Things that I would think important or even things that weren't. Right now anything of value would surely help.

When Mr. Santos returned a few days later, we went over all the information that we had gathered so far. It didn't seem like much to go on, but he said he was going to see what else he could come up with. He also said not to get my hopes up just yet. I told him I was beyond that at this point, but that I would keep my fingers crossed.

It took about two weeks before I heard from Mr. Santos. When he came to see me again, he had found out where all the evidence and the stenographer's information were located. There was a warehouse that held all the dead and closed court case files and documents that had to be kept. These items were never to be destroyed. It was located in the Bay area. Actually it wasn't too far from where I had worked. Herman told me that he would go through it all to see if anything could be found that would be of use to us.

It was like I said before: Herman Santos was the best at what he did. When he returned to the prison to see me he had some good news that might help us: he had the court files and stenographer's pages. All the original paperwork, indictments and history of the proceedings; the only thing that wasn't there was the desperately needed gun. The good news was he found hidden in the back of the box what was probably what we needed to have. It was the transcript and the fingerprint results taken off the gun. They acknowledged that the only prints on the gun were of the owner's, Sal Molino. We could go with that, but if we could get ahold of the gun it would be easier.

Mr. Santos and I finalized our plan. He would go to the judge to know if he would see him about the missing item, the gun! Then we would know how to get things rolling.

Mr. Santos went and found the Bay area address of the judge. He introduced himself and asked the judge about the missing gun, but was told that he didn't know what Mr. Santos was talking about. He also indicated that he didn't know of any missing items from the case.

Herman and I knew that the judge was lying, as it was a known fact that the judge had a collection of various items kept as souvenirs from different cases. Herman and I decided that we would just have to go with what we had and prayed that it would be enough to free me.

Now all that was left was to get into the court system for a new trial. Herman let me know that the new evidence did give us a better chance at clearing my name.

Herman left after telling me he would see to getting a court date. Hopefully it wouldn't take too long. After Herman left, my spirits seemed to be lifted, from all of the good developments and effort that was put into gathering it all.

I started to feel that I could possibly see the outside world once more. We would immediately file for the new trial in light of all the new evidence that we unveiled. A friend of mine, Pete, was to be paroled soon and told me to get ahold of him if I was released. He gave me the number of a bar that he frequented.

It took around two weeks for Mr. Santos to return with a court date, set for February 19, 1984. That was two weeks from that day. Mr. Santos and I spent hours going over all the information that we had accumulated, which would be necessary for us to prove that I was innocent of the crime of murder. It shouldn't take too long because we didn't need a jury for this case. All that was needed was the judge, my lawyer, and me, of course. Also needed were the prosecutor's office and the stenographer, and the bailiff. The trial lasted about two weeks and ended March 5, 1984.

It was about lunchtime when all the evidence was presented to the judge. He called for a recess but added that he had to look a few things up and come back with a verdict around 2:00 p.m. I wasn't very hungry but figured that I should eat something, so Herman and I went to the restaurant across from the courthouse.

When we arrived at 2:00 p.m., we had to wait for the judge to arrive. Neither Herman nor I knew what to expect. After a few minutes the judge arrived and called the court into session. The judge stated that he tried to figure out what kind of court of law had convicted me back in 1957, but it definitely was not the right kind of law. That I was definitely being violated of my rights from the beginning; all of the new evidence which we had presented proved beyond a reasonable doubt that I was innocent and should be released. The judge also stated that he was sorry that I spent all of those years in prison for nothing. He then asked me if I wanted to file proceedings against all who were involved in the case of The State vs. Jake McFarland. I thanked the judge but replied that I had enough of courts and lawyers for a lifetime. The judge laughed at that and said that I was to be released as soon as possible. After I was released, my record would be erased. Again the judge said that he was sorry for what happened to me.

As we left the courtroom I thanked Herman and I wanted to know if there was anything I could do for him. All he said was that I should try to renew my life again. All that I could answer was that I would definitely try. After the case I returned to the Q. and waited for my release to come through. I knew that it would only take a day or two at the most.

On Thursday March 7, 1984 I was released from prison. This would be a red letter day in my life. Now that I am finally released, I had to get myself reestablished to life all over again. I needed a place to live and I needed a job. When I was released I received a check for over $17,000 from what I earned over the years; I really didn't use much in prison except for hygiene and health products. I found an apartment right away in the town of Greenbrae not too far from the Q. It was a nice little furnished studio apartment, all the room I needed minus the familiar bars. I opened a checking and savings account and purchased a used automobile just right for me to get around with.

I had a phone installed and I started to look around for work. I was going to try to get a position in my field but knew that would be hard, because things have advanced since I had been in prison. So I applied for whatever I thought I could manage for now. Mostly I looked in sales. It was a week or so before I heard anything; it was for a shoe store in the area. I went down and spoke with the manager. He offered me the job after saying that he would try me out. The pay was $125.00 per week plus commission on my sales. Being that it was Friday he said that I could start on Monday. It wasn't really what I wanted but it was a start. The hours varied: three days 9:00 a.m. till 5:00 p.m., and two days 10:00 a.m. till 9:00 p.m. closing. My days off were Wednesdays and Sundays. After about a month or so I felt comfortable being back on the outside. At first, everything seemed strange to me seeing how the world advanced over the years.

Chapter Ten

Starting a New Adventure

I figured that it was time to get hold of my friend Pete, who was paroled not too long before my release. Pete did ten years out of a fifteen-year stretch for armed robbery. Pete told me that if I ever got out to look him up. He also said that if I ever needed anything, and he meant anything, I should get a hold of him right away. Pete had told me of this bar that he frequented. I figured that I would surprise him.

I dropped by the bar and asked if Pete was around but was told that he hadn't come in today. But the bartender added that they actually never knew when Pete would pop in. I decided to stay for a few drinks myself since I was already there. The bartender brought me my drink and said that Pete comes and goes, no regular routine. I said, "Thanks, I'll hang out for a while to see if he drops by." After a couple of hours I decided to leave. I paid for my drinks and told the bartender that I probably would stop by again tomorrow evening.

I did stop by after work as it was one of my early days. When I entered the bar, sat down, and ordered my drink, the bartender told me that Pete would be stopping by in a little while. I thanked the bartender. I thought I would wait around and have a couple of drinks while waiting for Pete. A while later I was watching the news when I saw the door open. It was dark in the bar but it looked like Pete. Sure enough I recognized him as he got closer. I waved and Pete came over to me. Pete smiled and I knew that he was glad to see that I finally had gotten out of the Q. He asked me how I was able to get released and I explained all that happened. Pete was amazed with it all. We talked and drank for a while when Pete asked if this was a friendly visit or if I needed a favor.

I told him that it was a friendly one but I did need a small favor also. He wanted to know what I needed. I told him that I needed a gun and that it needed to be untraceable. Pete wanted to know what it was going to be used for.

I explained it all to Pete and he said that it was a real stupid idea. All I could answer was, "Probably, but I really need one." I added that I was only going to use it as a prop anyway. He finally said that he needed about a week to come up with one. Sometimes what I needed wasn't so easy to come by. After about five days Pete called me and told me to meet him at the bar the next day. He had my package and I should come by about 8:00 p.m.

I spent most of the week thinking, planning, and plotting what I would do and how I would do it. That seemed to be a job within itself. I arrived at the bar a little early, but I did see Pete sitting in a booth at the back of the bar. I waved and approached the booth. I sat across from Pete and ordered a round of drinks for us. We chatted a bit while drinking our drinks when Pete reached under the table with a brown bag. He told me to check it out, and to be careful. I nodded and looked into the bag. There was a caliber 38 special in it and it felt loaded. He asked if it was okay and I nodded. We finished our drinks and ordered a couple of more rounds apiece. We were ready to leave when Pete asked me again if I was sure of what I was about to do. I just nodded and said to myself that I hoped so.

The first person on my list was Judge Albert B. Conklin, who lived in the Bay area down in Broadmoor. I studied his habits, including times of his going and coming. I watched who came and went it was mostly mail deliveries and paper boy deliveries. Nothing out of the ordinary or unusual; he had rather a dull life to say the least.

After a few weeks I felt that everything should run as planned. I figured that now would be the time to go and see the judge. I thought of something I heard in a movie a while back, wherein someone said, "It's a good day for a killing." That seemed to fit my agenda to a tea.

I drove down to Broadmoor and parked my car in front of the judge's house. I sat there for about ten minutes thinking of what I was about to do. I guess my conscience was kicking in. I finally shut off the car and walked to the judge's house. I rang the bell a couple of times and waited for what seemed like ages, yet it was only a few minutes. He finally opened the door and asked who I was and what he could do for me. I pulled out the gun and pushed my way into the house, closing and locking the door behind me. He said that he didn't have any money if that's what I wanted. He didn't recognize me at first, but finally realized who I was. He told me that he already told the lawyer that he didn't know anything about the gun or its whereabouts.

I told him that I knew all about his collection of items and other pieces of evidence that became missing in the outdated and closed cases that he had presided over. He asked me if I was going to kill him with the gun I was holding. I said no but if that is what it's going to take to get the gun in my case then I definitely would use it.

The judge wanted to know of what importance the gun was to me anyway. I replied that the gun cost me twenty-two years of my life, so I think that I earned it. After some time he finally decided to give me the gun. He went over to a special safe hidden behind a false wall. He opened the safe and brought out the gun. He handed it to me saying that it had no value whatsoever. I just looked at it remembering that night so long ago. The gun felt a bit heavy, meaning it was still loaded with the bullets. The judge smiled and said, "I thought for sure you would kill me with your gun."

I produced it and said, "You mean this gun? Oh, no! I wouldn't kill you or anyone with this gun, but I will kill you with this gun that wrecked my whole life when you wrongfully convicted me of murder which I didn't do. Now you know the value of it to me." With that said I fired the gun and the judge fell to the floor. I really can't say how I felt. I never actually killed anyone before. I sort of felt a bit numb yet filled with anxiety all at once. I did know for sure that my revenge was now a reality. That was when a feeling of justification flowed through me like a freight train.

So many thoughts were going through my head. I knew I had to leave very quickly but my body denied me of the movement, as if I was frozen in place. I snapped out of it shortly then went to my car and left knowing that this wasn't the end of it. My revenge will have to be finalized before I could feel whole again. One dead and three more to go.

I drove to the bar and saw Pete. I sat down with him and ordered drinks for both of us. I shook off a chill as it came over me. Pete asked me if I was okay. I told him yeah, that I just felt a little cold. He said, "Someone just walked over your grave." What a fitting statement. I told Pete what had happened and he understood. Pete asked me if I ever killed anyone before. I answered that I hadn't. After I left the bar I drove to my place. I figured that I would wait a few days to see if the murder was reported or not.

After about a week later there was a small article in the paper. It stated that a retired Judge Albert B. Conklin was found murdered during an attempted robbery at his home. It mentioned that he had quite an odd collection of weapons found in a six-foot-high safe built into the wall of his den. All the items from the safe were impounded by the police pending investigation.

I bet I could tell them where a lot of the stuff was from, but I guessed I will let them figure it out for themselves. I sure didn't want to tip my hand at that point. They would only want to know how I knew about the safe and all of its contents. Then they would probably figure out who I was and about my interest in it all. My life didn't need any more excitement than it already had. I now had to think of who would be my next victim on my short list. In the meantime I had to get on with my life in general. My daily routine was work, eat, and sleep. I realized that being out of prison after all of those years life would be a lot more hectic than one would think. It sure wasn't easy to adjust to it again. You have to understand I had no family to speak of and no more friends anywhere. I was a loner except whenever I saw Pete. He was about my only friend. When I was inside I was alone in my cell, but during daytime you had friends to talk to or work with. You were too busy in the day doing one thing or another. The nights while you were all alone all you had was your thoughts good or bad. It was soon that the murder of Judge Conklin wasn't even mentioned. You didn't hear any more of the safe and the contents. I guessed it was like nothing ever happened.

Chapter Eleven

Second on the List

My daily life seemed to be going okay. The job was going good. I figured that it was the time to check out my lawyer Robert F. Goodwin next. The first thing I had to take care of was to see my boss about having some time off. I already had Wednesdays and Sundays off. I would ask for Monday and Tuesday. That way I could have a four-day holiday so to speak. I approached the boss and explained that I needed a few days off. Her asked me when I needed it and I said possibly a few days next week. I told him the two days and he said it would be okay as it was pretty slow at this time of the year. "Anything special?" he asked.

I replied, "No, just needed some time off; just want to look up an old friend."

I wanted to use the time off to my advantage that was for sure. I also wanted to see what Goodwin was doing now. The first thing was to try and make reservations. I called various motels in the Stockton area for the dates that I needed. I found a couple of them that would be convenient for my purpose. I asked if I needed to pay in advance to hold the room and was told that a deposit would do the trick. I then called a second one for Tuesday to stay overnight and would leave Wednesday afternoon after the deed was done.

I drove down Saturday night after work. The motel was on the outskirts of Stockton, which was fine for me. There wera a few restaurants around and also a few stores if I needed anything. After I checked in, I looked up the lawyer in the yellow pages and it appeared he was still in the business. I bet he would be surprised to see me. That's if he still remembered me. If he did remember me, he probably would want to know what I wanted after all these years and how did I get out of prison?

After breakfast I drove over to where he lived, figured that I would do a little surveillance of his activity. That is if he did anything or went anywhere. After an hour or so he went to the store and returned. Then he went out again for the newspapers. As I sat there my mind started to think about my children as I watched parents going by with their own. I didn't really know where they were or how they had grown. I wondered if my son had favored me or not. I also thought of my daughter and wondered if she had gotten her looks from her mother. Lord knows I missed out on a lot of my life while I was in prison. Watching the lawyer as he went about his daily routine, I thought that his life was as empty as mine was.

Monday came around and I thought that I would follow him around a while. He stopped at his office for a while, and then he went to the courthouse. He probably had a case going on. I thought that I should see him in action knowing that he wouldn't recognize me after all these years. Court started around 9:00 a.m. The case wasn't that big of a deal, possession of a stolen vehicle and substance abuse. As the day progressed, I noticed Goodwin was the same raspy and mundane lawyer that He was so many years ago. He seemed like a person who appeared not be too knowledgeable of the case he was presenting to the court. I thought to myself, *No wonder I lost my case.*

I was young and naive while he was my lawyer. It seemed as if he didn't do his homework. The day drew close to end just as Goodwin's case did. The person was convicted. I wondered what kind of winning streak he had. I probably would be doing the world a favor getting rid of Lawyer Goodwin. I followed him to a small bar on the strip. He sat in a far corner at the bar. He ordered a scotch and water with a twist. For no rhyme or reason I ordered the same.

I sat and sipped my drink slowly while I noticed that he gulped his down and ordered a second one. He finished that and ordered a third. I continued to sip my drink and watched him as he finished the drink and got up to leave the bar. I finished my drink and left the bar also. I followed him to his place and watched him enter the house. I drove back to the motel and retrieved the gun.

I drove back to the lawyer's house and sat for a few minutes to get my head clear. I wanted this to go as quickly and quietly as possible. I knocked on the door knocker but got no answer. I knocked a couple of times before the lawyer answered the door. He had the TV a bit loud and didn't hear the first knock he said. He asked me what I wanted. I told him that I needed some information on an old case of which he was the appointed attorney.

"But do you need a lawyer yourself?" he asked.

"No," I replied, "just some information concerning a case you lost in the spring of 1957."

He thought for a few minutes and remembered. He asked me why I was so interested in that particular case. "I didn't have enough experience to win that case. I failed that client. He really deserved a better lawyer than I was at that time."

"Well, why did you take the case if you didn't feel that you were ready for it?"

"I was trying to make a name for myself. I figured that if I could win a big one, it would make me well known and I would then really be on my way up."

"So you tried a case that you knew you couldn't win, all the while ruining a man's life forever."

"Yes, I still have dreams over that case."

"Well, you now can be free of that worry."

"What do you mean?" he asked me.

I pulled out the gun. I told him, "Now I will have my life back."

He looked at me and at the gun wide eyed just as I shot him.

I left his house and went back to the motel. With two down and two more to go, I'd rest for the night. I wondered if old Goodwin would really be missed.

Chapter Twelve

Prosecutor Next

After I left Stockton, my thoughts went ahead about the trip to Fresno. I knew that I would have to wait awhile to see what the news would be from my recent episode. I arrived home tired and figured I should try to get some sleep. Well, sleep came staggered on and off as my mind kept racing. All night I was restless and sweating. As morning came I felt just as tired as I did last night, but I had to get myself together and head out for work. As I entered the store, my boss asked me how my time off had gone. I replied that the things I needed to get done were completed. I got back to work and the day seemed to drag by. Not too many customers came in, which left me a lot of time to think about my next endeavor, the trip to Fresno.

I started to think about when and how. The days went by with no news about my recent accomplishment. To me this all seemed like a second job. I knew that it was wrong, but I also knew that it had to be completed no matter the cost, and the reality of it was I really didn't care. I felt at times that I was on a road going nowhere.

I went to the bar one night to see if Pete was around and he was there. Pete seemed to be the only person that I could talk freely to. I knew that he could relate to my problems. I told Pete all that has been going on lately. He said that I definitely was playing with fire. I said, "Pete, I know that, but it needed to done. I couldn't rest until it was finished, no matter what it would cost me. Even with my life."

With that said we sat and had a few more drinks. When we left I told Pete that I would see him soon, not knowing if that was true or not. I figured that now maybe I could get back into my regular routine for a while. All the time I would be planning and plotting my next moves.

The store seemed to be a little bit busy for a while, which helped to take things off my mind for a bit. I knew that I would go crazy if there wasn't anything to occupy my days with. While my days seemed busy, my nights now always seemed lonely once again.

My thoughts of Fresno occupied my lonely nights most of the time. I recently saw a small blurb in the newspaper stating that a lawyer in Stockton was shot in his home within the last week. Robbery didn't seem to be the motive. Oh well, just another person that would not be missed. The prosecutor, now that would probably cause a stir. But then it would be a shame if I had gotten caught while doing it or fleeing the scene. I thought to myself that if an upcoming detective figured out the whole scheme of my mission, I could get caught before it was all completed. That, I thought, would be my only dilemma.

I had to think of Fresno plus my flight to Italy, which would be my end game. Yes! Soon my ordeal would be finished as soon as my ex-wife was out of the picture. Now the search for the ex-wife's whereabouts would be an ordeal all by itself, but it needed to be done to complete my ultimate goal which would definitely be complete satisfaction of a job well done. All I knew was that she lived somewhere in Italy. I also knew that she was remarried to someone connected with the mob. Well, back to Fresno.

I knew that the prosecutor would probably be in court all day, so with him I had to really be careful and come up with a plan. Also, it had to be timed perfectly. I did know that he was married with two children, both grown up and probably married. His wife I really didn't know about, but I was sure that wouldn't be a problem. He had to be in his early sixties by now. But no matter, there shouldn't be room for error. I figured the trip to Fresno should be soon.

I had to check out the court's daily dockets for the month that is if one was posted. I had to see the kind of case load he had within the next few weeks. I thought that I would drive down there after work on Tuesday and return Wednesday evening so that I would be ready to go to work on Thursday morning. I figured that I definitely would have to leave the States as soon as my dealings with the prosecutor, realizing that someone would put two and two together. They might think that there was some kind of connection to it all. There was a real need for completion, and that wouldn't be until my ex-wife was dealt with.

I told my boss that I had some family business to take care of on Wednesday and would return back to work on Thursday. He said no problem, he would open up the store for me that morning. After I left work, I went to the apartment and packed my overnight bag. On a hunch I for no reason whatsover found myself adding the gun. I didn't even know why. Maybe it was just an afterthought. I left it in the bag, then I had some dinner and drove down to Fresno. After driving a couple of hours, I spotted a vacancy sign at a motel close to Fresno. I figured this would be a good place to stay the night. I wound up sleeping late and woke up around 10:00 a.m. After I dressed and had something to eat, I drove over to his house and checked out the area. It seemed to be quiet enough if I had to do it there. I figured that I would drive to the courthouse.

When I arrived there, I found the docket board and looked for his name. It seemed he had quite a caseload. He surely seemed to be a very busy prosecutor. He had a case going on that day, so I figured I would sit in on it to see what he was like now. It should be interesting to watch the man in action knowing full well that he was a main part of my sentence.

I presumed he would now be getting paid in a way he never would have expected to. My next move was to plan my trip overseas as soon as I had gotten finished here. I needed a place to stay and figure out how long it would take to find out where she lived and also what things she did and when she did them. I realized that his schedule for the next Wednesday was an easy one. He had one case in the morning and another case in the afternoon. That seemed like the only day I could have a chance. I figured I would be able to do it after the afternoon session was over. Before I left, I wanted to hang around in the parking garage to see just where he parked so I would be ready for the kill. When he came down I stayed in a darkened area of the garage and watched. He went a bit further towards the other side of the garage. I watched as he entered the car. After he drove out and left the garage, I went and looked it over: it had his name on the parking space as did the other employees. I figured now I knew where I would have to be positioned next Wednesday afternoon.

I drove back to my apartment and went to sleep; I had to go to work in the morning. While I was driving home, I thought about the upcoming events and I figured it all out by the time I arrived at my place. After I got to my place, I called Pete and asked if it was possible for him to see if he could find out the whereabouts in Italy of my ex-wife and whom she married. I knew that I probably would need to know her name. Pete told me to meet him Sunday afternoon at the bar. I told him thanks and hung up. The work week went pretty quick. Sunday, Pete called me and said that he had some information for me.

We met at the bar and had a few drinks. Pete told me that her married name was Giovani. She lived in a small town outside Catania. Her husband was a part-time hitman for the mob, nobody of any importance. I asked him if he had heard anything about my children. He replied that he didn't find out any news about them.

Well, at least I finally had something to go on that was better than nothing. We sat and chatted some while we had a few more drinks.

We mainly discussed my trip abroad. I told Pete that after I took care of the prosecutor on Wednesday, I would drive to San Francisco and take the flight from there to Catania International Airport. The flight would take around fourteen hours. I would stay at the Best Western Hotel Mediterranean outside of the airport. "Before I go to the airport, I will first meet you here at the bar. I need one last favor from you. I know I can't take the gun on the plane with me. I hope that you have a way to get it to me at the hotel." Pete said he would work out something; it should be no problem. I was happy to hear that. I finished my drink and told Pete that I better get some rest for work tomorrow.

I slept a little better that night knowing that it would all be over soon. I had a few things to take care of before Wednesday. I had to close out my bank account, get my plane ticket, and pack. I figured that I would stay at the hotel until I found a place of my own. It could be a small house or an apartment, which was all I would need. I realized that I would only have a two-day week this week, but I would keep that under wraps. Morning came and I got myself ready for the day. First I had to stop at the bank and close out my account. Next stop would be the travel agency to book my flight to Italy. Then it should be about time I got to work. The bank wasn't too crowded so I was out of there in about fifteen minutes. The bank said that they were sorry to lose my business. I told them I was moving abroad for some family business.

Now the travel agency took a bit longer. I finally got a one-way flight leaving Wednesday night at 11:00 p.m. I would be cutting things close with my having to stop at the bar to drop off the gun, but I could manage it. I then went to work. The boss greeted me and asked how things were going. I told him that everything was fine. Well, Monday seemed to drag on by. Hardly any sales to speak of; after work I started to pack up for the trip. I really didn't have too much to pack. I knew that I had to remember to give both guns to Pete. I also remembered that I would have to call the hotel and make arrangements for my room. I called the hotel and asked if I could have a room for Thursday evening for about a week. That was no problem. Now all my arrangements were done. I could rest easy for now. Tuesday went about the same as Monday went but I made it. At closing the boss said, "See you Thursday." I just said "Okay" and left. I went home, ate dinner, and went to sleep. Tomorrow would be a very long day for me. I didn't have to leave too early to get to the court.

I got up around 9:00 a.m., made breakfast, got washed, shaved, and dressed. After a while I decided to load the car and take a walk for a bit to clear my mind. I called Pete and told him I would meet him about 9:00 p.m. at the bar. He said he would be there. It was about 1:30 when I decided to drive to the Fresno courthouse. I should get there a little after 3:00 p.m. I arrived at the courthouse around 3:15 p.m. I figured that I would get down to the garage and in the position where I would be able to finish the prosecutor. I parked around the block so I could just leave without being noticed. Hopefully no one else would be in the garage. It all looked quiet to me so I just waited. After about fifteen minutes I finally saw him coming. I waited till he got to the vehicle when I approached him. I said, "Excuse me, maybe you can help me?"

He said that he hoped that he could. I asked if he remembered a case from 1957 in San Francisco when he convicted a man for murder. All he said was, "Vaguely. Why?"

I replied, "I was innocent."

He looked at me then he looked at the gun. That's when I shot him. He fell to the ground dead.

I quickly left the garage and went to my car. I sat there for a bit. When I heard the sirens, I figured that I should leave. I drove back and went to have something to eat at a restaurant. I later went to the bar to wait for Pete to come. It was about 9:00 p.m. when I saw him come in. He came over to our table and sat down. We talked a bit and had a few drinks. I gave him both guns and left, saying, "Goodbye for now."

Chapter Thirteen

The Awaited Trip

After I left the bar, I drove to the airport and got myself ready for the flight. I got there about 9:00 pm; the flight was leaving at 11:00 p.m. The flight would take 14 hours; we should arrive at the Catania airport early the next afternoon. The hotel was right near the airport, so that wasn't a problem. I figured that I would be able to sleep on the flight to Italy. When I arrived at the airport, I checked in and had my luggage loaded. I figured I would go to the lounge for a few drinks.

I stopped short of the lounge thinking back to my intended flight so long ago. I hoped that it wouldn't be déjà vu all over again. No, I didn't think so. I was thinking foolishly now. I had two drinks and they were calling for my flight. I think my heart was in my throat while I was approaching my gate. I didn't see any agents or anybody out of the ordinary. I slowly walked towards the boarding area looking around and not seeing anything or anybody out of place. I continued and handed my ticket to the stewardess who said that I should have a good flight. I thanked her and boarded the plane. After I got in my assigned seat, all I had to worry about was that it wouldn't take off when it was scheduled to. I still had the fears of the past. I guess I won't feel comfortable until we were in the air. Finally, liftoff! I guess I was safe enough to get some sleep. Yes sleep did come, seemed I slept the whole flight. The next thing I heard was "Put on the seat belts." That they were ready to land in Catania airport; after I got my luggage, I took the jitney to the Best Western Hotel. It was a huge hotel. I checked in and a young man took my luggage and escorted me to my room. You could say it was more like a suite. It had everything a person could ask for. It was a shame I wasn't there for better reasons.

After a good night's sleep and a bit of breakfast, I decided to rent a car to travel around with. I still had to wait for a package to come. I might enjoy the sights of the city and countryside. Maybe later I would get in some swimming. I figured that I could get a decent tan while I was sort of vacationing. Then later I would take in the nightlife. The week went by and I sort of was getting used to the good life. When I got back to the hotel, I was told that a package had arrived for me. I went over and picked it up, thanking the desk clerk. I went right up to my room.

As soon as I got to my room, I was like a kid on Christmas morning opening the presents. I opened up the package. There sitting wrapped in soft white paper was my instrument of revenge. Sal Molino's gun; I bet he would never have thought his gun would be getting this much use. Well, back to reality. I now had to get serious: vacation time was over. I would drive to where Grace was supposed to be living, somewhere around the city or town of Lentini, about 35 miles south of Catania.

I drove to the town of Lentini. Upon arriving, I located the postal office and went inside to find out the whereabouts of a Mister Garret and Grace Giovani. They looked it up for me and said that they lived south off Strata Stat ale 194; then turn left on via Enna to the last villa a little outside of the township. I figured I would drive around the area and see what was going on. I wanted to see where Grace had wound up. It seemed to be a large villa surrounded by trees and was fenced all around. There were no neighbors around them. I saw a big pool in the back. She sure had a nice place. I guess she finally got what she wanted–but I was going to make sure she got what she deserved. I had just one bullet left in the gun and her name was on it. I knew that I would have to figure it out as soon as possible. I really didn't want to blow it by getting caught at this stage when the end was near.

As I looked around, I saw that across the road was an area with a lot of brush surrounding the whole side. Apparently it was a vacant lot. I noticed that I could drive the car in the back of it and not be noticed. From that point I would be able to see the whole villa and watch what happened and when people came and went without being noticed. Now that's taken care of, all I had to do was figure out how to proceed.

I drove back to the hotel and checked about house rentals in the area of Lentini. I left my phone number with the local realty office. I explained that I wanted a small furnished cottage for myself while vacationing in Italy. After a couple of days the realty office called to let me know that they had a small cottage available. It was furnished and I would be able to get it on a monthly basis. I told him that I was definitely interested in it. He asked me to meet him at one o'clock that afternoon and we could look at it.

I went to the office and the gentleman took me to see it. The place turned out to be a little bit north of Lentini. Also it was on the 194 road where they lived only a few miles south. I told him I would take it as is. I had to pay the rent and a month's security. I moved in the next day and figured I would be able to start my watch in a few days after I got settled in. It was a cute little place and close to some stores, which was a plus all by itself; I went for a walk and picked up some groceries for the house. I saw a bar across the street and figured that I would enjoy a few beers. They served meals so I got a cheeseburger and fries. It didn't taste bad at all. I had a few more beers and then went back to the house. I also picked up a pair of field glasses while I was shopping, figuring that they might come handy.

It took me about a week to settle into my new home. I got used to area it wasn't as bad as I thought it would be. After I felt comfortable enough, I figured that it was time for me to start my research for my last ordeal and resolve it to the fullest. I drove to my little alcove across from Grace's property and made myself as comfortable as I could.

I watched the comings and goings in and out of the place; mostly it was mail and paper deliveries. Some people visiting came and went. It wasn't until a few days that I noticed that Grace was driving through the gate. She drove a Mercedes. I guessed she did all right for herself after all. I started a log of arrivals and departures for each day; it would take Grace a couple of hours when she went out and returned. Grace really didn't go out too much. When I did see her go somewhere, I also noticed that she really looked about the same just a bit older. As I mentioned she didn't really go out much, maybe twice a week.

After Grace returned, I figured that I'd call it a day. I drove back to my house and wondered where my children were. They were grown now. I wondered if they lived around here and were they married? How did they make out for themselves? If only I could find them and see what they were like and how they were doing. I wouldn't let them know, but I figured that I shouldn't take the chance. I guessed I should stick to my plans taking care of my ex-wife and be over with it. The only thing that kept haunting me was that I was once married to her. Also, I once loved her. Oh, how I loved that woman!

After watching the comings and goings from their property, I noticed that Grace mainly went out on Wednesdays. I figured that I would approach her the next Wednesday. All I had to do now was figure out how I was going to do it. Would I be able to go through with it? Still I keep remembering how much I loved her a long time ago. We were married and had two children together. I had to get control of myself. I couldn't keep dwelling on the past that has been gone for so long.

Well Wednesday finally rolled around. I had a good breakfast and prepared for the day. I checked the gun to make sure I still had a bullet in there. Everything seemed okay so I left for her place. I got there and drove past her place knowing that she always turned left. I pulled over to the side of the road, popped open the hood, and waited.

I finally saw that the gate was opening and her car appeared. I looked under the hood as if I was looking for the problem. She pulled up next to me and opened her window asking if I needed any assistance. I answered, "No, ma'am, I think it just overheated but thanks." I asked her if she was Grace McFarland. She smiled and answered that she was Grace Giovani. I replied, "Oh, you look a bit like her," but she added that many years ago her name was Grace McFarland but that was her ex-husband. I stopped her then and said, "I know, Grace." She looked at me as if she now recognized me, and that was when I fired and shot her. I watched her die before I left.

I returned to my house and thought that I would lie low for a few days and find out what would be said about the murder. There had not been anything in the papers. I kept looking, then one evening on the news it was mentioned that a prominent woman, Mrs. Grace Giovani from the area, was shot in her vehicle. No suspects were apprehended. It remained under investigation. They didn't know why or what happened. I just had to wait it out. The next few days I tried to relax and enjoy my solitude, but my mind kept running over what I had done. What I needed now was closure, but that didn't come either. My mind was still racing over it. Out of the four killings this was the hardest. I figured that I should call Pete and let him know what was going on.

Chapter Fourteen

What's My Next Move?

I called the bar and asked the bartender if Pete was there. He said Pete just come in. I told him this was a long distance call and could he please get ahold of him for me. Pete got on the phone and we talked for a bit before telling him that I had finished up my problems, but that I couldn't get it out of my mind. My thoughts always go back to my killing Grace. Pete said that he knew that it was going to happen. He told me that was the guilt setting in. He added, "Your main problem will be learning how to live with yourself. The first three killings were different. They were people that you really didn't know personally. But with Grace it is another story: you were married to her and had two kids. Those are things you can never get over no matter how much you try. You're going to have to learn to accept it all. Then you have to learn how to live with yourself. That is the hardest part. Good luck, my friend."

We chatted for quite a while before we said our goodbyes and hung up. My conversation with Pete didn't help too much. That part about trying to live with myself, just living is hard enough without doing it with what I had done in the last few weeks. As the weeks went by it didn't get any better. I knew that I had to do something, but I just didn't know what to do or how to deal with it.

Another two weeks and I still didn't see any news about the killing of Grace or even if the investigation was still ongoing. Maybe if I heard some news I could settle down a little. What they say about no news is good news is a lie.

I rationalized my options. I could go on living the way I was but all the while I'd always be looking behind me to see if I was being followed. I could be arrested or shot. Sooner or later my luck would run out. I could always run again, but run to where? No matter where I went sooner or later I would have to run again.

I was to the point where I just had to talk with someone and the only person I trusted and knew was Pete. It seemed that whenever I had to get back in touch with the outside world, Pete would be there. Again I put a call into the States. The bartender answered and I asked for Pete. He knew it was me so he said, "Wait a minute," while he located him. Pete got on the phone and asked if I had a problem. I assured him that I didn't but wanted to talk to someone familiar for a change. I knew that he definitely was suspicious when he wanted to know if I was okay. We chatted for a bit. Pete sounded really good on the phone. Talking with Pete was the only thing that seemed to keep my sanity intact. We talked for quite a while before we said our goodbyes saying that we should keep in touch. I always seemed to feel better after I talked with Pete for some reason. Pete became a sort of a crutch for me, generally able to help me with decisions if and when I asked him, but this one I couldn't really involve Pete. He would probably say it was a bad idea.

I finally realized what I needed to do. The only thing left for me was to turn myself into the authorities, specifically the local police department. I'd explain that I just murdered my ex-wife a few weeks back. Her name now was Mrs. Grace Giovani. She was Mrs. Grace McFarland when she was married to me in the past. This was the best plan that I could come up with. The one thing that I believed was that the United States was looking for me with three other capital offense murder's. A judge, prosecutor, and another lawyer.

That would be my ace in the hole, so to speak. I knew that they would have to extradite me to the United States. Trying to sleep was useless as I was very restless knowing what I was about to do. But there wasn't any other outlet for me. I don't even think prayers would help at this point. I had something to eat for breakfast then tried to figure out my next move. I figured that when the bank opened for the day, I would take out around a thousand or two to keep me in necessities for a while. Later I could have the rest of my monies rerouted to a bank wherever I landed in the California penal system. I really didn't know if I could really do this so I drove around for a while. This wasn't the easiest decision that I would have ever made. Turning me into the police didn't seem to fit well, but I guessed that was my only option at this point. I drove around for what seemed like hours before I went to get it over with.

I finally drove to the police station. I went in and walked over to the officer who seemed to be on duty. He asked me what he could help me with. I said that I wanted to report a murder. He told me to wait while he called a detective to come down and help me with the details. A gentleman approached me and asked me what I wanted. I explained that I was reporting a murder. He asked me who was murdered. I told him Mrs. Grace Giovani. He looked and repeated, "Mrs. Grace Giovani." I told him, "Yes, I killed her."

He took his gun out and called for another detective. He told the other detective that I just walked in and admitted that I had killed Mrs. Grace Giovani. The other detective wanted to know why I wanted to kill Mrs. Giovani and how I killed her. I then told them that it was owed to her and that I shot her with a caliber 38 revolver.

"What do you mean that it was owed to her?"

I told them that she was my ex-wife.

"Well, I guess we will have to book you. She is, I mean she was a prominent citizen here, you know."

I went through the booking procedure once more. I told them my name was Jake McFarland; that she was Mrs. Grace McFarland a long time ago and we had two children, a son named Thomas born in 1949 and a daughter named Felicia born in 1950. We were married in 1948. They ran a check with my prints locally but came up empty. I told them to run a check through Interpol for three unsolved murders in California around the San Francisco Bay area. A report came through of three unsolved murders that seemed suspicious and still open involving three people murdered with a caliber 38 revolver, including a retired judge, Albert B. Conklin, a prosecutor, Jason Gibbs, and a lawyer named Robert F. Goodwin.

They asked me where the gun was and I told them it's outside in my vehicle in the glove box. One officer left and returned with the gun. They proceeded to book me for the murder of my ex-wife and locked me up. They contacted the police department in San Francisco and informed them that they were holding a person of interest to three murders in the state. One of the officers came down to the cell area and told me that the States were sending an agent to pick me up. It would be about four days before he arrived.

I really didn't mind the wait. Besides, the food there was pretty good; when the agent arrived, it took a few hours to get all the paperwork completed. The agent asked me if the retrieved gun was the one used to kill the victims. I acknowledged that it was. I also told him that it was the same gun that I was convicted with in 1957. The agent told me his name was Melvin but that I could call him Mel. He informed me that we had an early flight for San Francisco with a layover at O'Hare airport. Mel also mentioned that he didn't think I was a flight risk due to the fact that I turned myself in and he didn't want to draw any unnecessary attention to us. That it would make for a better flight. After a while Mel said he had to check into the motel and that he would see me in the morning. I didn't know if I was having a period of regret or a sense of satisfaction that soon it would all be over. I was once more restless and couldn't sleep too well until morning came. It seemed like it would be a nice day. The guard came and let me know that I could get showered and shaved, that breakfast would be in shortly. After I cleaned up and had breakfast, the agent arrived to pick me up. We drove to the airport and checked in for our flight. After we boarded the plane and took off, I was ready for a nap. It really was a long flight as I remember it. I was awoken by the stewardess asking if I wanted lunch. I asked her how we were doing time wise. She replied that it was on time, but we still had a while till we get to O'Hare. The lunch seemed pretty good for flight food. I gazed out the window and the weather looked clear. That always makes the trip more enjoyable. I dozed back off again I guess for a few more hours. I awoke as we were pulled into O'Hare airport for our layover so we just walked around and found a quiet restaurant and went in for dinner. There wasn't any hurry so we took our time and talked about anything that came to mind, staying away from talking about my situation.

Chapter Fifteen

Back in San Francisco

The plane landed in Frisco around 7:00 a.m. the next day. It was foggy as it usually was with mornings in San Francisco. After we landed and had some breakfast, I asked the officer if we could stop at the bank to have my money transferred from the bank in Italy. He said that it would be all right. We stopped at the bank and it took a while for the paperwork and the transfer to be completed. After that I was escorted to the city jail where I would be housed awaiting court proceedings. All of the jailers were different now, being that it's been about twenty-eight years since I had been there.

I would be housed in the city lockup close to Alcatraz. I would probably be moved to the Q. awaiting my execution once I have been sentenced. The officer did at least give me a good report from our trip, stating that I was a model prisoner on the long trip. They processed me with my fingerprints and all else that applied before I was brought down to my cell. I noticed that the jail system hasn't really changed that much.

After I settled in, I felt a bit tired so I lay down and took a nap. I was awoken by the officer bringing my chow. I was told that it would probably be a week before I went to court. I replied that at least I won't be going anywhere. I thought that maybe I could put a call into Pete and maybe he would come down and see me. I called the bar and asked for Pete. The bartender noticed that I wasn't calling long distance and confirmed if I was back in the States. I said, "Yes, but can you please call Pete to the phone for me?"

Pete got on the phone and asked me where I was. I told him that I was back in Frisco. He asked why I didn't stop by the bar. I told him that I was in the city jail and asked him if he could come visit me on Sunday. He asked me what was going on and I replied that I would explain it all to him on Sunday. He asked if I needed anything and I said I didn't need anything, just a friend to talk to. He told me to hang in there and he would see me Sunday. I told him goodbye and then was escorted back to my cell.

On Sunday Pete came to see me and we chatted a bit about what if anything was going on in his life. All seemed to be okay. After a bit I started to explain to Pete my situation. I told him that I just couldn't live with myself any longer. I found that I couldn't sleep or do anything else. My remorse and guilt was all I seemed to have left. Pete said that he knew what might happen to me with all that I was doing. He figured that it would create problems in my life, but that was something that I had to deal with myself. All that anger that had built up in me finally took over.

I told Pete that I know what he was saying but I did what I had to do. Pete said he understood. After a few hours he asked me to let him know when I had to be in court and he would be there for me. I told him that I would definitely give him a call. With that said and done we said our goodbyes. I was then escorted back to my cell.

On Wednesday I was informed that I had a court date set for Monday at 10:00 a.m. I called Pete and told him the day and time. He said He would be there. Monday arrived before I knew it. I knew I didn't need a lawyer because I had turned myself in and confessed the crimes.

When I arrived at the courthouse Pete was standing there, which made me feel a little better. The other people who should be there were the judge, prosecutor, and the court stenographer.

As I thought, the trial lasted about 30 minutes. The judge asked me if I had anything to add on my behalf before he set the sentence. I said the only thing I would want is to request that I be put to death in Alcatraz. The judge asked if I realized that Alcatraz was closed already and I said yes I did realize that but I would like to be electrocuted where it all started. The judge said that the only one who would be able to okay that would be the governor but that He would get ahold of him and find out if it could be done. I told the judge that I would cover the cost if that was the problem. The judge convened the court until the governor approved or denied the request. He would get back to me with the answer. Then the judge conferred with the prosecutor and both agreed to my request. I was sent back to the jail to await answer.

It took about a week before I heard from the judge again. Back at the courtroom, the judge said that the governor agreed to my request. It was then that I was convicted for four counts of murder in the first degree. Ironically the date was May 22, 1985 Friday, just twenty-eight years after my first conviction. I was to be sent to San Quentin for a period of ninety days to wait for the preparation of my execution to be held at Alcatraz. After I was brought back to the jail, I called Pete and told him that it was set for ninety days and had to wait for the setup at Alcatraz. I added that I would be sent to San Quentin in the morning. Pete said he would come to see me for a while. Well at least I wouldn't have to go through the orientation process again as I did the first time there.

I slept rather well that night. When I awoke I got dressed and breakfast came shortly after. It was around noon that the police escort picked me up to take me to Quentin. The drive would take an hour. I sat back and watched the scenery. It was a very pretty day for a change.

When we arrived at the Q, I breezed right through because I was considered a special case. The warden greeted me, stating that he had wished he wouldn't have to see me back, especially under these circumstances. I couldn't agree with him more. He told me that since I would be there for a few months, he would let me work in the library. He understood that I knew my way around the books.

I thanked him for remembering, saying that I would go bonkers if I just had to sit around all day. The time went by as it usually does in prison. Three meals a day, work, and some yard time. There generally were movies on Sunday night unless they got cancelled for some reason.

Pete came to visit me as he said he would and I enjoyed them. He would tell me about things that went on at the bar mostly. We also talked about my decision. It was good for me as it made the time go easier. I saw a couple of guys I knew who were still here, so I had a few people to talk with. They gave me updates about life in the Q since I left; all of it was irrelevant to me but I listened anyway. You know, just prison garb, like who went to the hole or who just got out of it. I really did enjoy my time working in the library where I could check all that's going on in the outside world on the computer.

The warden came down with some news about my execution: it was tentatively set for September 23, 1985 at midnight. The cost to me was $12,000 for all the extra things to be done for my request. That I didn't mind. I wondered why they always wanted to do it at midnight. I realized it's because of the extra energy required: it was safer as the city was asleep mostly and no businesses were open. That way there would be no power outages. Having thought that out made sense to me; I called Pete as soon as I could to let him know what the tentative date was. He said okay and that he would see me on Sunday.

I tried not to dwell on the past too much, but every once in a while it crept up on me. But thinking of the happier days always seemed to work. My time kept getting shorter. I still had a lot of sleepless nights, but that seemed to become the norm for me. Now that my day of doom was getting closer, my mind seemed to play tricks with me—what if I did this or what if I didn't do that?

Or what if I didn't do any of it, would my destiny be the same? I started to think about my children and what they could be thinking about me or if they even thought about me at all. That is something that I probably will never know. It was the end of May. My time was coming to a close. Pete came to see me again. He asked me how I was doing. I told him that I couldn't wait until it was finally over. When Pete had to leave, he told me that he would be there with me at the end.

Chapter Sixteen

Coming to My End

The day after Pete left, I had a strange visit from a Mr. Gary Saltwell. Gary introduced himself and told me how he became interested in my case after picking up the story of the three murders in the Bay area. He told me that he really couldn't find out too much about the case but that he continued to search on his own time. For some reason he figured that they were all related but couldn't work out the details until he found out that someone was being sent back to the United States after confessing to them. It was said that the person had murdered someone in Italy but also confessed to the three murders here. After I arrived back in the United States and went through the court process, Gary said that he wasn't allowed in the courtroom because of the sensitivity of the case. No reporters were permitted in for the trial.

After I was sentenced, Gary followed me to San Quentin to speak with me. He mentioned that he had worked for a local newspaper and became interested in my case. He was doing research on the three murders in the Bay area in the early part of 1984 but always came up short with the answers until now. Gary finally asked if he could write a book about my story.

I agreed as long as he would find my children and share the profits if there was any to be had. He told me that he would write up a contract from my requests and together we would sign it. Then it would get notarized and I would receive a copy. He also mentioned that the warden gave him a daily pass so it would be possible for him to get all the information that he would need for the book.

I soon narrated my life to him from where it all started, with my marriage to Grace. Gary would arrive in the mornings and left around sundown. Some days Gary brought lunch for both of us. That was definitely appreciated considering what was served for lunch at times.

I really started to enjoy Gary's visits; he was an interesting young fellow. One afternoon Pete showed up for a visit. I introduced him to

Gary and I explained what he was doing. Pete thought it was a good idea for so many reasons. After that, all he could say to Gary was, "No pictures, no pictures!" We all laughed. It turned out to be a very interesting and fun day for a change. After a while Pete said that he had to leave for a previous appointment, adding that he just wanted to stop by. He confirmed that he would see me soon. I asked Gary about his job, wondering if he would get in trouble. He said that he took some personal time off to stay focused on my story. I came to respect that about Gary.

Pretty soon our daily sessions came to an end. Somehow time seems to fly by when your mind is kept occupied and June just seemed to fly by. Here we were into July. Gary told me that he needed a week or so off to take care of some personal business; it seemed odd to me because of all the time Gary has spent with me, I never even thought of him having a personal life.

Well, to tell you the truth my brain needed a rest. At this point I felt that Gary knew more about me than I did. Time seemed to slow down while Gary was away. I sort of felt lost without his daily visits.

I dreamt that night about my end: in it, I was on the trip to the Rock. The trip down from San Quentin was about 18 miles going by the ferry. That would be the quickest way to the Rock. I remembered my first trip to Alcatraz from the city's lockup back in 1957. The ferry would take the children to the mainland for school. Their families lived on the island. Other employees who lived on the mainland would also be going to the Rock for their day's work. I was going there for my sentence. I smiled to the children as they waved to me.

But this trip would be different in so many ways, there would be no smiling and waving children; no employees going over to the island for their tours; the buildings wouldn't be all lit up. Although the dock would be lit up awaiting our arrival, on the dock the warden and the priest would be waiting. As well, the entrance to Old Sparky (Electric Chair) would be lit up. I heard a rumor that no one has ever been electrocuted there, making me the first and probably the last. That would probably be some sort of honor if you could call it that.

On the trip down to the Rock there would be only two guards, myself, and of course Gary Saltwell. Oh, I almost forgot the ferryman would have to be there. That is if they still called them ferrymen. I was awakened by the morning whistle. Wow, I thought that was real. It was only a dream of what was to come soon enough.

The day started off as usual *first was* breakfast, then the yard which was followed by the daily work detail. I strode down to the library and to my surprise Gary was already there. I sure was glad to see him. I asked him how things went. Did he get everything settled? Gary told me that everything had been resolved. I really didn't know what we were talking about but was glad it went well for him.

Gary was raring to go. He was excited that we were nearly finished with the book. August was a very hot month, which was the norm for August. All that was left was the ultimate and inevitable end of one Jake McFarland. When it rolled around to September Gary and I were both mentally exhausted, yet we were excited about the book. All that was left was to add the execution then he would get it published. Gary told me he had a publisher who saw some part of the book and was very interested in it. It sure was exciting; who would have thought that would happen?

I saw Pete one more time before the big day. He was saddened that I wasn't going to be around to visit anymore. I also knew the emptiness that had come between us. I tried not to think too much about what would soon be the inevitable. I started to think about my children. Thomas would be thirty-six years old and Felicia would be thirty-five around this time. I wondered if they still knew of me or if they ever thought about me.

I had about a week left when Gary came to see me. I was always happy to see someone from the outside. He seemed to be in deep thought so I wondered if everything was all right. He assured me that all was okay. He did mention that the publisher really thought it could become a best seller. That was good news. He told me that the warden informed him that we would be leaving at about 9:30 p.m. for Alcatraz. I asked him why so early and he said he really didn't know. It seemed odd because the scheduled time was midnight. The one thing I was happy about was that if the book sold like they said it might, and if Gary did find my children, they would benefit also. I would die a happy man knowing that as a father I would be able to leave them something I really think might come in handy for them. Well with one week left to live, there wasn't much that I could do at this point but wait it out.

My daily routine wouldn't change that much. I did enjoy going and working in the library; that at least kept my mind occupied for most of the day. It was the nighttime that was always the hardest for me. Alone in your cell if you weren't tired, all you could do is think until you drifted off. My last week now had me thinking of my life more and more it seemed. While in the yard some of the other inmates intimated that they were glad not to be in my shoes at this time. I had to really agree with them. This wasn't really the place that I thought I would be in at this time. Life can really be cruel at times.

As the days got closer, the warden stopped by to see if everything was all right. He wanted to know if I needed anything. I said that I was fine just trying to wait it out the best I could. He left saying if I needed anything to let him know. I said, "I will see you Monday for sure." By the end of the week I was a nervous wreck. Sunday afternoon they announced that there was a movie for the night; the thought of it made me feel better. It meant that I could relax for an evening outside of my cell.

Monday morning went as usual. I wasn't really hungry at breakfast, so I just went to the yard. I went up to a few friends and said my goodbyes. Then I went down to the library because I was too nervous to just hang around. By lunch I felt a little better so I went to lunch. It wasn't bad. By the time dinner came around I had to eat in my cell. I had steak with fries both smothered in an onion and peppers gravy. For dessert I had a whole pie ala mode for myself. After, the warden came down to see me to let me know that they would be leaving at 9:15 p.m. I asked why so early? He told me it was because a storm was coming. It had me wondering. When he left I sat there trying to think of better times. It didn't work too much.

The guards came down to pick me up and had me sign some forms. They were mostly papers about my belongings; then the banking forms for my children if they could be located. If not, the state takes possession of them all.

Gary did arrive and we boarded the ferry. There was the warden, a priest, and two guards. Oh, let's not forget the ferryman. It was a quiet and peaceful night on the water. When we arrived we were greeted by the executioner.

Together we all walked to the building. In the quiet night one could hear the music from a bar across the bay. When we arrived the warden explained the procedure. The priest was doing his thing. Gary tried to be casual but you can tell he was nervous. When we approached the area where Old Sparky was, we sort of took a turn the other way for some reason. We arrived at a big room and went in. There I saw Pete with a smile on his face. That took me by surprise. I went to Pete and shook his hand. A door opened behind me and a couple came in. I had to do a double take. Right there in front of me stood my two children, now grown. They ran over to me and hugged me, coming to me and calling me "Dad." It made me the happiest man in the world.

I looked at Gary and Pete. They just shrugged their shoulders and smiled. Now I realized that this was planned all the while. I looked over to the warden and he just nodded and grinned.

I spent about two hours with my children. We really had to get to know each other in a short time, but this was all that I could have hoped for. They forgave me. They knew all about. It Gary had filled them in. We had a good visit, but the time came up sooner than we realized. I kissed them both good-bye and hugged Gary and Pete.

As we walked to Old Sparky, I held my head high with a smile on my face. When they strapped me into the chair and readied the switch, the warden asked me if I had anything I wanted to say.

All I could think of was, *My life is now complete....*

www.ingramcontent.com/pod-product-compliance
Lightning Source LLC
Chambersburg PA
CBHW071247020426
42333CB00015B/1664